THE WINGS OF MORNING

See how the trees move

Under the wings of morning

Free from the night voices

Mingle bird songs

And children's laughter

Above a kite

Glides on the friendly breeze

Below pigeons flirt

In endless skirmishes of love

A ceramic goose

Gazes silently

Across an endless lawn

FIRST GIRLFRIEND

After the rain

The sun

Sat grinning in the puddles

People talked

Some happy

Some sad

And the shoppers pushed

And struggled

Through the world's muddle

I stood there

Waiting

The sun above

Laughed at its own jokes

I saw her

Long before I spoke

And my mind hurt

As I walked to her

Through the world's muddle

CORNISH MEMORY

Sweet Summer days

When life was dreamtime

And falling in love was easy

On sheer cliffs, on heathered moors

Or underneath a granite Tor

Or lying close within

The sandy sun-drenched dunes

Then cooling off

In sea as clear as glass

That ran light green over the sand

Beneath a blue dome sky

We walked through marram grass

That fringed the malachite sea

Heady with spray and the smell of her hair

I died in her deep green eyes

DIFFICULT CHOICE

Two temptresses one dark one fair

Sweet neat bodies cascading hair

Amenable I found to my soft line of talk

Both willing it seemed with me to walk

'Twas agony to choose which beauty to befriend

But they preferred each other

Though as we three lay that night entwined

Together under the smiling stars

I suppose

It really didn't matter in the end

HAPPINESS IS A PRELUDE TO CONTENTMENT

Amber solace

From the Northern bleeding sun

Amber hair, eyes blue

As days begun

Lithe sunburnt memory

Of death of my desire

With her short catch of breath

EVEN TODAY

Even today

They sing

Evening spreads

Its wings over the dead

The sacred mountain

The Chinese garden

Paper thin

Even today

BEAUTY WITHIN

We sat part circle

Another boring meeting

She across the room

Not here before

New uneasy

Her downcast eyes knowing

Most saw her as unattractive

Suddenly

In my mind a voice

"All are precious to me"

Precious she

I acknowledge her

And as I looked

Her face, body, being

All lit up

Transformed

She looked across at me

And smiled

WITH APOLOGIES TO ANDREW MARVEL

DNA screams make more of me

Dawkins tells us it's OK

So come on baby do it now

I can happily show you how

We should enjoy each other just tonight

Tomorrow is sure to be alright.

I could waste a lot of time

Convincing you that now is right

So may tomorrow never come

Now is the moment to have fun

Driven by their DNA

When darkening night has cloaked the day

They make their own hay

Thoughtless to consequence

They may by accident create

Driven by desire too strong

To just stand back and wait

Lovers unable to anticipate

A future which lies unseen

Not always the way they hoped

Their future might have been

ROSAMUND APPEARING

At the foot of the stair

I stumble

Unprepared

Fall into a future dream

In the hall standing

You

Transfixed

Incoherent

I hurtle towards

What was always meant

Though never imagined

Until that moment

DREAM JOKING

No longer to play

The dream-joking game

Look sweetly between

The still gazing air

What did we used to say?

Nothing but a name

Where floating lily-thoughts

Sway upon each stare

Now

Newly awake we lie

Flower light still plays

Dancing in your hair

THE ENTANGLEMENT OF LOVE

The satanic urge dictates desire

Which makes men powerless

To admire

How truly lovely is a woman

No slave

But she by her own choice

Can play the willing partner

For one who comprehends

Her overwhelming beauty

And happily conjoins

Two souls held as in a quantum state

By the entanglement of love

That in an instant spans the universe

Mocking the feeble speed of light

Not bent by gravity

They sail through time

Their ragged lines of destiny

Running together

Wires in the singing rigging of romance

SITTING IN COMFORTABLE SILENCE

Sitting in comfortable silence

I listen

As your words weave colour

Into the fabric of a story

Enraptured

Gazing across our table

I see your face still so clearly

As though you've never left

Your tales, like Scheherazade's

Paint tessellated pictures in my mind

Your love reaches out across the divide

Smiling gently

CARDBOARD HORSES

Cardboard horses

You would say as we drove past

They were always there

Stoically savouring their last morsel

Before moving on to delight in another

Of equally succulent delight.

I always sensed your desire

To swap souls with them

Longing for nothing more complex

Than their undefined future

Their serene contemplation of nothingness

Yet I'm glad you remained

That forty four years with me

ROSAMUND LEAVING

There is nothing I can think or say

Only emptiness, a void that cannot be filled

I never wanted to achieve this hour, this day

This place, this time I would freely yield.

How compressed the days, the months, the years

From our first moment to this now

Everything within the worldly sphere of time

Eternity alone has space to grow

But we were pulled together by the gravity of love

The speed of light I know

But who can guess the speed of love

That issuing from God's heart

To those below

Sustains us in a way we cannot prove

EVENING SLOE HILL

The light is darkening

Sounds subside

Calm spreads across the lawn

Ashen sun

Rubs on motionless trees

Upturned faces of drowsy flowers

Look skyward

Echoing the scents

Of yesterday

PEACE ETERNAL

Unexpectedly It hit me that Sunday

Peace which the world cannot give

Past all horizons

At the true centre

I floated timeless

Suspended

Space stretching wide on every side

Without end

Calm joy

An eternal moment

Beyond the edge of existence

Being and not being

Longing to rest

In that place for ever

Your dying words to me

"It's alright"

And then again

After a space

"It's alright"

Did we both touch

Though differently

A sacred moment.

Finally, alright for you

And still awaiting me.

HOW TO FIND YOU

So many souls

Since the dawn of time

Wandering bemused

In heavenly bliss

But where are you?

Such a crush

Reincarnation requires

Reinvention

At least cremation

Has deleted kilograms

Of cumbersome body parts.

But reborn

In a new heavenly body

Yet still recognisable

I should know you

We didn't arrange a rendezvous

Like just behind the Holy entrance gate

Nor did I post in advance

The time of my arrival

But prompted by the carol's descant sound

I will seek you with God's children

All in white

Waiting round

MIDNIGHT SKINNY DIP

A deep dive

From moonlit rock

Slice through the surface

Into inky blackness

Darkest purple cloak above

Beneath

Wrapped in airless embrace

Held suspended in a cold grip

Floating dreamlike

Until lungs bursting

Feet and arms thrust

Towards the surface

Emerging

With gasping indrawn breath

Floating amazed below

The star-pricked velvet dome of night

BEYOND THE FIELD OF MARS

Deep velvet purple night

Breaks through to day

Earth

Caught by blinding light

Spins on its way

Suns dance galactic gyres

Light years away

Reborn from cosmic fires

Black-eyed quasars penetrate

The Milky Way

Here on this planet

This tiny crowded earth

We struggle every minute

To uncertain futures

Evolution limping forward

Billions of years since birth

What might we gain

If we could stray

Beyond the field of Mars

Is there less strife

Is there less pain

Amongst the distant stars

DAMN SEAGULL

Perched upon roof tiles guarding your chicks

Swooping to attack

Suspected threat

Just visitors to my front door

Aloof on seaside lamp-posts

You dive

Suddenly

To steal an infant's chips

The locals hate you

Cursing God

Demanding the purpose

Of your Creation

Yet I see you sailing on the wind

Of a storm from the southwest

Wheeling

Diving from the zenith

Screaming with joy

In the blustery squall

Alone

And in concert

An aerobatic ballet

Lit by the sun

Evolution forged you

Just to have fun

IN A MOMENT

Cool mists

Of summer mornings

Greet the dawn

Of blistering days

Anticipating

We pause wondering

Then driving onwards

Desperate to achieve

Rush headlong

Ignoring pain

Caught between

Now and next

Finally

In a clear moment

We see

Timelessly

The lost may still be found

Faithfully

Dreams remain

Following

The hot stillness of a summer's day

Comes

The gentle taste of rain.

IT WILL BE ALRIGHT IN THE END

Though none can see

Beyond the bend

Why do we all say

It will be alright

In the end

Young lives that strive to grasp

The furthest galaxy

Pledge eternal love

Dream a perfect future

Though they cannot see beyond the bend

Swear hearts allegiance

Till the end

Men in their prime

Clever in politics powerful movers

Taking our world so close

To the ultimate brink

Though they cannot see beyond the bend

Stupidly believe

It will be alright

In the end

Old men at end of day

Full of history and pain

Slowly spreading through their frame

Though they grow weaker by the day

Still find the strength to say

It will be alright

In the end

If each could see beyond the bend

They might perhaps pause

To think and then to say

It might be alright

In the end

OLD PHOTOS

Images drifting

Yesterday's thoughts

Your voice your face your kiss

Lingering

Sleeping impassive forms

That will not move again

Evading firm grasp

Refusing to be pulled close

Ghostly dreams

So hard to grasp

To tear back from time's

Distant retreat

LAMINATOR

I had a terrible ordeal

With the laminator

She said

Henna hair

Tumbling down her straight back

Live the dream

I replied absently

Awaiting patiently

The arrival

Of my laminated card

And she walked away

Into her tomorrow

TOMMY

Tommy was our tortoise

Of amiable nature

Small constrained within

His bulky shell

With a delight of

Dandelions

To be devoured starting

At the stalk

Until at last

The golden-headed flower

Seemed itself to devour

His very face

A mystical

Golden faced

Four spiny-legged beast

Until with one final gulp

He became Tommy again

NOVEMBER 2022

Sad lady in the square
As I pass by
Full of my own moment's joy
Suddenly
My soul is heavy
With the world's grief

I paused to say a word
Acknowledge her
She told me little
Simply said thank you
That I had stopped a moment
To recognise her grief

I walked on
Inadequate
That I could do so little
For such sadness

Don't we all feel so bad
Knowing this pain ever
Touches someone
And we can change so little
Only pass by

LOLA GLOWING BRIGHT IN BANGLES

Lola glowing bright in bangles and a multiplicity of rings

Sweet unassuming gentle caring

A muse

To whom this poet sings

Hoping nightly to explain

The incomprehensibility of things

Wild bats that flitter through his brain

Trigger false meanings with their wings

Yet still a certain truth he seeks

Below the quantum world it speaks

In a strange tongue about a truth

Only a poet can explain

Lola's kind and gentle greeting

Calms a rambling crazy brain

Lends a warmth to any meeting

Bringing peace and rest again

May a future free of strife

Be written in her book of life

INTERVIEWER'S INTERVIEW

Are you the right person for this job

They ask repeatedly

Someone with kindness

Gentle skills empathic questions

An eagerness to share

Can you extract from some poor suffering soul

The every detail of their pain

Pin down precisely

The loss hurt anger desolation grief

And share this bathos

With your captive listeners

And having achieved

This gruesome task

Brightly announce

There'll be good news

After the weather forecast

TREEFALL

Rooks circle noisily above

Discussing a wind-broken tree

This frozen February morning

Killed by greedy ivy

Half fractured from the trunk

Finally torn by a seasonal gust

The rooks shout to each other

They are pleased

They did not choose this tree

But preferred its fellow

A sturdier ash

Still Clasping

The nests they built with care

Last year

To which return begins early this season

THOUGHTS LIKE FISHES

Thoughts like fishes

Swim through the mind

Most

Spawned from earlier days

Floating lazily

Others more recent

Eagerly dance with anticipation

Creation cannot pause

Ideas evolve

Against the entropy of time

Relentlessly

Give birth

To yet more complex theorems

Fate reveals

New opportunities to change the past

Time to have fun

Things to be done

Till the earth rolls up its pages

And the book is closed at last

PERSISTENT MEMORY

Deep green eyes of passion and abandon

Ecstasy of youth

Sempiternal love it seemed then

Yet for so many long years

The quiet contentment of family

And children and grandchildren

A different consummation

More fulfilling

Now you are no longer here

Those younger hedonistic years

Are just yet the siren call

Of a more distant past

Before ever I saw your face

A CERTAIN SADNESS

A certain sadness walks with us through life

Anxious to whisper in our ear

Between the transitory joys and laughter

Things are deeper than they appear

The burden of continued days grows quietly

Against the ebb and flow of time

Nurtured by the soil of each experience

Weight added day by day

To innocence

AN APPLE A DAY

It's not my fault

She was the one that gave me that bloody apple

Suddenly

A lightning bolt of insight

I started at my every thought

Striving to distinguish good from evil

Testing the logic of my mind

With truer knowledge of myself

I struggled in a mental dance

What should I be or should not be

Conditioned by inheritance

Moulded by an outside world

Yet somewhere deep inside of me

The knowledge I was free

Now we have a new machine

To think for us

With artificial electronic dreams

Magnitudes greater and more swift

Its algorithms unlike the patterns of our minds

Whose insights were the apple's gift

As yet it has no insight

Cannot tell us in what way it solves

The problems that our maths evolves

Presently it seems to serve mankind as lord

Its superhigh intelligence

Working mindlessly

But it may only lack an apple

Itself to be free

SUDDENLY

Suddenly

All changes

Not far

But far enough

And worse

In the wrong place

From those who love you

The eternal question

Asked continually

And today's now

Becomes uncontrollably

Immediate

Encountering the world's

Hard edge

Quite unexpectedly

No Zen

No cry suffices

To the bright blue

Hemisphere of God

Only grief

Gives lie

To all human hopes

And fears

All virtues and all vices

THE BRAIN THAT HIDES WITHIN

The brain that hides within

Makes its own decision

The eyes that peer without

Show no concept of vision

The mouth that curves below

Smiles smoothly with derision

Should I believe this man

Place my faith with him

Let him guide my hand

Believe I'm freed of sin

Admit humanity should be

Equal and thus happy

Or

Perhaps

Pause

And wonder why

So many

Since the dawn of time

Knew the answer

To make it all fine

And yet

    And yet

We have so much sorrow still

To regret

THE CAT-LIKE SUN

The cat-like sun

That stalks and jumps

Around the ragged shadows

Cast by broken gates

Languidly embraces

Stumps of trees

That though once noble

Now are dead

Climbs higher

In the sky

Enshrouds the earth

In its great cloak

Of incandescent light

Finally descends

To drowse

With melodious bees

In the blue lavender

Scenting the early evening

The darkening light of day

Calls to the night voices

Awakening dreams

To swim between the stars

WAITING

Waiting

Nothing of interest around

Inside

Teeming thoughts

Hammer within the bony dome

Seeking freedom

Such incarceration

Should focus

Concentration

But the brain

Lacks control

Tedium

Infuses Heaven's Departure Lounge

Coronavirus delays escape

To more desirable resorts

But could perhaps

Expedite

A last-minute flight

From earth

RAIN TODAY

Rain Today

My window gazes

On another morning

The grass revives

Under metallic light

Of a grey domed sky

Time limps slowly forward

Through the eternal now

A moment

The last and first

Of one more dawning

Must it be

Always thus

This unrequited yearning

Longing

To leave

LATE SUMMER

It is dull overhead today

Pink faces of roses upturned

To catch the feebler light

Trees caressed by wind

Birds retreat

Until more clement times

Sunlight filters

Through grey-black clouds

Seeking the life it must sustain

Giving energy

To integrate the whole

Brain and limbs

Flexing together

HYMN TO THE GOD OF BLOOD

Satan loves religion

His favourite place to hide

Burrowing down inside a mind

That believes it prays to God

Turning love to hate

Gentleness to pain

Believing its own god delights

Each time a sinner's slain

Yet one day we'll awaken

From the world's dark nightmare dream

At last in truth we'll see The Light

Inneffable serene

Then beg for resurrection

From the eternal burning lake

Claim a new direction

Perhaps too late for escape

LOCKDOWN BLUES

(?BY AN AGED MICK JAGGER – Who still can't get no satisfaction)

We can't find our cerebration

We have lost the power to think

Locked in here creates frustration

Pretty soon we'll take to drink

Life in here is no tonic

It requires a lot of gin

Our boredom is something chronic

We are far too old to sin

Everybody's so kind to us

All the staff are very nice

As long as we don't make a fuss

Or indulge in some dark vice

Each tomorrow, every sorrow

Drifts away from us too fast

Can't remember last December

Was it Christmas in the past?

DEDICATED TO MINNIE

WHAT DO SWANS THINK?

I wonder what swans think

you said

As we walked together

To the point at Blakeney

Your voice, your question

Still lingers in my mind

Like so many

In the forward rush of time

Bleak thoughts like black rooks

Wander the wet grass of morning

Beneath the naked trees

Seeking comfort food

Words evolve

Endless phrases since time began

Deafening bewildering, sounding all at once

All creation screams together

The clamour grows relentlessly

Like entropy within vast silent space

Yet in between the billion galaxies of words

Can yet be heard that still small voice of calm

REAL REALITY

There is a reality

Immeasurable

Inaccessible to research

Underlying existence

Deep calm extensive

Fundamental

Beneath random quantum states

Undefinable by equation

Embracing all things

Above below beyond

Impossible to grasp

In mental concept

Yet known to many seekers

Whose minds reach out

Into the stillness

Deeper than the Chaos

Eternally exists

The creative love of God

THE LAST AND FINAL POET

Sailing softly Westward

The last and final poet

Gazed back upon

The wake of his voyage

A sea of verses

Tumbling like waves

More words than in the myriad galaxies

Appearing through the dusk

Of evening

Words of his own

And every fellow traveller

Of his trade

Striving to explain a truth

Which even poet's language

Scarcely comprehends

In gathering darkness

Life's short dreams

Finally become a new reality

ROCK ANTHEM *(With Power Chords)*

Incarceration

Immolation

Total frustration

Life in chains

Isolation

Deprivation

Desperation

Blows my brains

Tired of waiting

Full of hating

Zero rating

Pushing down

There's no exit

Can't make the chords fit

All my strings are

Out of tune

Out of sorrow

This existence

Ended soon

THERE STOOD A TOWER

There stood a tower

Some many miles inland

Tall and built alone

By unknown hand

Examined o'er the years

Its height width composition

Detailed by architects and engineers

Gave no clue regarding its position

Though every brick

Composing window, alcove, door

Was scrutinized in detail, inch by inch

Down from the top to underneath the floor

But why the sages asked

Build this in such a soul-less space

An edifice so far away from anywhere

In such an unlikely place

None could discern the reason

For why that tower should be

Yet its builder once a sailor in his season

From this tower's top though far inland

Could still though distant gaze upon the sea.

BRIEF MOMENT

Brief moment

A sigh

A Breath on the thin parchment

Of life's parable

Each transitory second

Of a sentient life

Extends forever

Shared

In a smile

In a kiss

In a prayer

Thoughts dance together

These moments

Forever alive

Have each a sacred page

In the unknowable cosmic mystery

AN OLD SOUL

Painted several years ago

In eighteen eighties France

A damsel with a tambourine

In a whirling dance

Soft eyes, pert nose

She gazes sweetly down

Is she perhaps an old soul

Who from a painting travelled here

To give a sweet smile to each stranger

As she pulls their beer

Perhaps in these old Angel Vaults

A new angel has appeared

HOW CAN IT BE

I truly believe I love you Lord

But somehow fail to see

How can such a perfect one

Love a wretch like me

I love some for the beauty of their eyes

Friends for their kindness

Others for humility compassion generosity

All such easily lovable qualities

But you know the very depth of me

Where sadly little virtue hides

Yet you persist unconditionally

To love a wretch like me

HOW CAN IT BE II

Because I am nought but crudely human

Born of violence hatred greed and lust

I ask how can it be

That you the perfect one

Can possibly love me

I dreamt a voice gave answer to this prayer

A calm argument of simplicity

God loves you for what you are not

Yet what God longs for you to be

A SATANIC VERSE

Satan screws up good intentions

Cleverly corrupts our mind

Leaves us to regret

Our actions

Leaving only guilt behind

Yet that devil is unable

To misdirect our prayers of love

Nor ever comprehend

The loss of one who kneels in grief

Seeking comfort from above

HEAVEN

(Inspired by "Somewhere" by Stephen Sondheim and Leonard Bernstein)

There's a place for us

A place in heaven for us

Free from sorrow and pain and care

We'll meet with Jesus there

There's a time for us

A time when we must leave

Say goodbye to lovers and friends

Going onward at our end

To heaven

Knowing that we are forgiven

We'll make our dwelling in heaven

Heaven,,,,,   Heaven....... Heaven

There's a home for us

A home in heaven for us

Joy at last after all those years

No more need for tears

Eternity

Our God at last with thee

We'll be free and blessed by love

In that place above

In heaven

We know that we are forgiven

We'll at last find peace in heaven

Heaven....   Heaven.... In Heaven

STAINED GLASS WINDOW

Fragment of broken colour

Where glass blinds

The narrow moment

Reflection of pain

In the insistent brightness

Now we see darkly

It is dark within

The penetrating light

Is chilled

Beyond the glass

Light dances

Made in the USA
Columbia, SC
01 October 2023

23678940R00050